ANOTHER DAY

Another Day

Sabbath Poems
2013–2023

❀❀❀❀❀❀❀❀❀

Wendell Berry

COUNTERPOINT
California

First Counterpoint edition: 2024

Library of Congress Cataloging-in-Publication Data
Names: Berry, Wendell, 1934- author.
Title: Another day : sabbath poems 2013-2023 / Wendell Berry.
Description: San Francisco : Counterpoint, 2024.
Identifiers: LCCN 2024010035 | ISBN 9781640096394 (hardcover) | ISBN
9781640096400 (ebook)
Subjects: LCGFT: Poetry.
Classification: LCC PS3552.E75 A87 2024 | DDC 811/.54—dc23/
eng/20240301
LC record available at https://lccn.loc.gov/2024010035

Jacket design by Nicole Caputo
Jacket photographs: landscape © iStock/Levi Schultz,
woodgrain © iStock/yasinguneysu
Series design by David Bullen
Book design by Laura Berry

COUNTERPOINT
Los Angeles and San Francisco, California
www.counterpointpress.com

Printed in the United States of America

1 3 5 7 9 10 8 6 4 2

This book is dedicated
with love, with thanks
to Mary and Steve

Then gin I thinke on that which Nature sayd,
   Of that same time when no more *Change* shall be,
   But stedfast rest of all things firmely stayd
   Vpon the pillours of Eternity,
   That is contrayr to *Mutabilitie*:
   For, all that moueth, doth in Change delight:
   But thence-forth all shall rest eternally
   With Him that is the God of Sabbaoth hight:
O thou great Sabbaoth God, graunt me that Sabaoths sight.

—from *The Faerie Queene*
by Edmund Spenser

Contents

2013

2014

❧ Contents

ANOTHER DAY

I.

This is a poet of the river lands,
a lowdown man of the deepest
depth of the valley, where gravity gathers
the waters, the poisons, the trash,
where light comes late and leaves early.

From the window of his small room
the lowdown poet looks out. He watches
the river for ripples, flashes, signs
of beings rising in the undersurface dark,
or lightly swimming upon the flow,
or, for minnows, descending the deeps
of the air to enter and shatter
forever the momentary reflections,
for the river is a place passing
through a passing place.

The poet, his window, and his poems
are creatures of the shore that the river
gnaws, dissolves, and carries away.
He is a tree of a sort, rooted
in the dark, aspiring to the light,
dependent on both. His poems
are leavings, sheddings, gathered
from the light, as it has come,
and offered to the dark, which he believes
must shine with sight,
with light, dark only to him.

II.

Times will come as they must,
by necessity or his wish, when he leaves
his enclosure and his window,
his homescape of house and garden,
barn and pasture, the incarnate life
of his desire, thought, and daily work.
His grazing animals look up
to watch in silence as he departs.
He sets out at times without even
a path or any guidance other than knowledge
of the place and himself as they were
in time already past. He goes among trees,
climbing again the one hill of his life.
With his hand full of words he goes
into the wordless, wording it barely
in time as he passes. One by one he places
words, balancing on each
as on a small stone in the swift flow
in his anxious patience until
the next arrival, until he has come
at last again into presentiment
of the Real, the wholly real in its grand
composure, for which as before
he knows no word. And here again
he must stop. Here by luck or grace he may
find rest, which he has been seeking
all along. Sometimes by the time's flaws
and his own, he fails. And then
by luck or grace he will be given
another day to try again, to go maybe
yet farther before again he must stop.
He is a gatherer of fragments, a cobbler

of pieces. Piece by piece he tells
a story without end, for in the time
of this world no end can come.
It is the story of eternity's shining,
much shadowed, much interrupted,
in time. And time, however long, falls short.

III.

In a country you know by heart
it is impossible to go the same way twice.
Changes of time, mind, weather,
and light make all ways new.
To one whose eyes have opened, any place
is compounded of places unending
to the end of time, and travel is well
accomplished by standing still.

IV.

The years have not brought him
the philosophic mind. The years
have brought him love and grief.
They have taught him that grief
is love clarified, appraised
beyond confusion, affirmed, lifted
out of time. No idea, no answer
has come to him to prove the world
and lay all trials and days
to rest. What comes is the light, dim,
almost substantial, of the oil lamp
in the middle of the kitchen table,
casting into the dark around it
the shadows of the old grandparents
and their small grandson at supper.
The three of them were a nucleus,
a part of life, within the light within
the warm room within the winter
dark and the wind within time,
the presence, that while they ate
almost in silence their frugal meal
carried them on from what even
the old ones only partly knew
to what they did not know.
Supper finished, the dishes done,
they prepared to go from the warm
kitchen through the cold hallway
to the front room where they would sit
by the stove until it was time
to build up the fire for the night
and go to bed. The boy, small
for his age but in ambition large,

eager for the duties of a grown man,
asked to carry the lamp. He wished
to be the one to light their way.
Perhaps in the dimming of their years
they wanted their way to be lighted
by him. They allowed him to lift up
the lamp in his two hands and go
ahead into the dark hall. The lamp
he held heavily away because
of the heat it breathed into his face.
The chimney rattled, and he reached
to steady it. It burnt his hand.
The chimney fell and shattered.
The flame, now unconfined, flared
and smoked. The old ones, frightened
now for him, for themselves, for the worn
old house and its immanent fires
that held them all alive, bent
to the boy. One took the lamp.
There came a tenderness then, rising
out of peril and their fear. They laid
their old hands upon the hurt
young flesh of the boy, touching
through time the life beyond
their lives. Tenderly,
tenderly, they instructed him
in danger. If he had dropped the lamp
with its live flame, its charge of oil,
the house surely would have burned,
themselves perhaps with it—even
he, their treasure and hope, gone
in the blaze, in the twinkling of an eye.
It was the tenderness of their knowledge
of the frailty of their being alive

together, for a time, in time, that held
then the three of them in the fluttering
smoky light, and it holds them
now forever in the mind of the boy
grown old: the two old ones bent
over him in such a terrible
tenderness. Now, their equal finally
in years, how he loves them, how
misses them. How carefully still
he holds them in his thanks.

V.

On the morning of the first day
the old shepherd comes early
to the barn and finds the last
of the season's lambs newly born,
safe, and thriving. It is the morning
also of the resurrection of Christ,
the lamb of God, His people's shepherd,
while the keeper of the timely flock
anoints the broken birth cords
of the little ones now breathing the air
of the cold day in the gray light.
He pens them with their mother, brings
hay to her and water, serving
again the communion older than memory,
truer than time. And so the highest
and the lowest stories are made one
in his mind in his work, clumsily,
difficultly as may be, day by day.

VI.

Here is the first fact
of the history of spring: you cannot
remember it as you go about
your chores in the winter cold,
the world and its informing
life dead in your heart,
or imagine it as it will be
when it comes fully into living
presence in light and warmth.

From nothing to lavender phlox
afloat in the air, to the leafing
oak, to the yellowthroat: the ancient
miracle realizes itself
again. The most factual
denier must think of nothing
before these somethings can appear.

*

Where the winter lay dead-brown
on the woods floor, now green
leaves and flowers open
and flourish in unconditional being,
recalling nothing, expecting
nothing, nothing guaranteed.

Like the flowers, I too
must live on without condition,
expecting nothing but to be
present in the passing day,

to the limit of breath living
as I humanly must and may.

Last summer another elm,
another of my old companions,
died of thirst in the relentless
heat, giving up its leaves,
and still it stands, passing
into life, a winter
scrawl in blossoming spring,
lifting up its perches
to the birds, while the season performs
newly its old work.

VII.

This is the daily gift
of birthdays and all days:
to see through the years
in the one present
the proved companion you are,
the girl you were.

4/30/13

VIII.

I think of us all at work
in our sweated clothes, the day
bright and hot, the rows
long. I think of our talk,
our laughter, and the silence returned.
Owen and Loyce Flood,
Melvin and Marvin Ford,
Reuben Brown, Eddie Sharp, Chloe
and Sis and Ed Poe —
from our time together
in this world,
I walked with them all
As far as their graves.
When I forget them
I won't know my name.

IX.

I came upon Mr. Hardin
standing in front of the courthouse,
looking up. "Son," he said,
"look *way* up yonder.
No! Up *there*." It was a buzzard
he wanted me to see,
a black speck *way* up
for no reason unless glory.
Some beings eat the dead
and inhabit the sky.

X.

Greatly troubled in his mind,
he went to a place in the woods
where not a leaf was moving
and under the trees the creek
was flowing without a sound,
a place as low in this world
as the water had worn, and the quiet
came down from highest morning,
as he knew, only to be broken,
but the while it lasted would stay
with him and comfort him
in whiles that would come after.

XI.

Admit us at last to Thy silence
which includes our own — our
greatly needed forgiveness, mercy, love
which have at last no speech.

And Thine is yet the greater silence,
the greatest, Thine only,
in which all commotions and all cries
subside, are hushed, and come to rest.

XII.

Waked up by thunder in the west,
I lie without moving, looking up
through walnut leaves at the sky.
Here the light is gray, but eastward
in the clear a sun-lighted
white cloud is standing almost still.
Wakened maybe by a thought
I had been dreaming, I lie as still
as the cloud, thinking of all
that has been lost in my lifetime,
not the many who have died,
but the substance of the earth, burned,
blown, or washed away,
the cleannesses of water and air
lost. And then beneath the thunder
the yellowthroat's small voice calls.

XIII.

Let us say there is no life after death
and you know for sure there is not. Let us
say you are dying and you know for sure
that you are, and you are seeing for the last time
this green pasture enclosed in the woods
and the sky of shape-shifting clouds,
a hawk crossing, a buzzard circling
high up and slow, the sheep flock
grazing at ease in the cool of the day,
the yellow flowers of summer's end
lighting around them, and the air alive
with the newest passages of small birds,
dragonflies, butterflies,
the hunting wasp flying home
with its prey. And you, now seeing all this
for the last time, as if for the first,
knowing as you always have known that you see it
only once, once for all,
in its one moment of ending and coming
to be, in its moment of shrugging off
the thought of ending, of becoming—you
see that you are no longer counting,
but have passed across into a place
you have never been, have always been:
new, a new earth, forever new.

XIV.

"For he is not a God of the dead, but of
the living . . ."

Luke 20:38

The old dog with her gray muzzle
and I with my fringe of white hair
please ourselves by nearness to the fire
inside while outside the birds answer
their calling to stay alive. We all
now have fewer days than we had
yesterday. But it comes to me
that I know at last how all of us
are held in the union, the communion, the assembly,
the great membership of this world's life
that comprehends its numberless
becomings and farewells. In the Kingdom of God
all who ever lived are living.
Only we humans, we the poor,
suffer the ancient mistake, dividing
the living from the dead, confusing life
with time. We divide life from death
for the purpose of killing each other, killing
ourselves, or we confuse living bodies
with machines, the truly dead, to increase
happiness and "create wealth." Hell
fills the difference. The wrens, searching
the brush for this day's food, rightly
give not a thought to death, singing,
as they live and move, the longest song.
The Kingdom of God is life itself.

XV.

To steady us in space
We have this given place.

Placed and timely, time
Offers the gift of rhyme.

We co-depend, you said.
So knowing, I thee wed.

XVI.

I wake in the dark
in the deep night
and the room is filled
with the smell of rain.

XVII.

Looking at screens,
listening to voices
in nonexistent distance,
seeing, hearing nothing
present, we pass into
the age of disembodiment,
the death of love finally
realized as we become
our pictures adrift,
homeless in placeless
space of the mind only.

XVIII.

Young love grows older,
grows old, accumulates
burdens. losses, failures,
griefs, but also the history
of itself lasting through time,
and so transcending time
as an image of forever
ever keeping, never old.

XIX.

The poet's question confronts
the poem, by way of the poem
the place, by way of the place
the world: How is it fitted
together? The question stands
and waits, to be asked and asked,
never finally to be answered,
which he believes affirms
a kind of faith. The world is
fitted together, is held
in its place in the great sky,
has held together so far,
through the worst of human damage
so far, and by no human's
power to save or make or know.
That he can sometimes fit
a mere poem's parts together
is his fallback position, a sign
of his limits, his formal ignorance, his
faith in the great coherence.

XX.

The lowlife poet moreover
is the poet of a "backwater,"
a "boondock," a "nowhere"
where life starts, yes,
from low down, but also
from high up, from the soil,
the sunlight, the falling rain
joining Heaven and Earth,
from his kept loves of friends
here and gone that also
are heights, their voices returning
to him in the darkest darks.
At night this lowly where
is reached by every visible
flicker of the heavens, to which
it is central, for it is the center
of the poet's half-lighted mind,
the only consciousness he has.
So it is his limitation
that gives due honor
to this place, seeing in it
the sanctity of all
creation in Heaven's sight.

2014

I.

The long cold drives life inward
into shelter, into the body, into
limits of strength and time.

Out of darkness day comes.
The earth now white, the trees bear
bright new foliage of snow,

beautiful, yes. "Beautiful, but hell!"
Junior Wright said, wading
in knee-deep snow to feed

the snowbound cattle. We were young
then and really didn't mind.
This morning, half a century

later, under the beautiful trees,
beautiful truly, repaying much,
I dig out the paths again,

renewing again the pattern of home
life grown old in this place
and many times renewed. Continuing

my difficult study, I remind myself
again: "Take no thought for the morrow."

II.

TO THE NATIONAL OVERSEERS

I am away in a quiet valley,
am busy at my quiet work
in this comely small cup of country
exactly fitted to my mind,
my mind to it exactly fitted.
It is enclosed by slopes and trees,
filled full of light and air and wind,
fulfilled by time and wear and weather.
My work is gathered of air and earth,
the history of the local light.
I am not going to tell you whether
or when I'm coming back. Don't wait.
Don't try to call. I have no phone.
There's not much left I want to shoot,
but I would like to shoot a drone.

III.

You don't know the day until
You've seen the last light
Reddening the hill
And rising into night

IV.

Having carried them within her
five months, and labored hard
to set them free, the fierce old mother
finds her lambs, wet from her womb,
breathing the cold air, struggling
on the soiled straw on the world's floor
to live, and she calls to them in loud
muttering gutturals of praise,
her absolute eloquence of joy, for they
who once were not, were nothing,
now are something, themselves, her own,
and her joy is at one with all joy
this world has known, and for the one
reason: The life that was not now is.

V.

The silence of the barn at evening,
when the shepherd draws shut the door
and starts home for the night, is heavenly,
for it says almost aloud that every ewe
has found her lamb and is content.

There is another of the barn's silences
that is heavenly also, for it says
that the ewes and their young ones
are gone from it away into
the now-green, the first-grown grass
of the spring, and they are delighted,
the shepherd delighted with their delight.

VI.

The mockingbird sings
his praises of his mate
or of himself. In his joy
he knows no difference.

At first I called him silly
and egotistical, like all
lovers in the spring,
unable to say enough
of his ambiguous delight,
and so he repeats himself.

And then I said, "He's right!
Love teaches him to fail,
at this best of times,
to know whose song it is,
hers or his."

4/30/14

VII.

The old man from up the creek
and the hillside woods got sick.
In the loneliness of his misery
he discovered he did not care
whether he lived or died. What
a relief! Much encouraged,
he lives, wandering long times lost
to all who wonder where he is.

VIII.

A SMALL PORCH IN THE WOODS

Why do you force the knowledge of me to leave your memory and go abroad, you in whom my gifts proclaim me who have blessed you with the right bounteous gifts of so many favours; who, acting by an established covenant as the deputy of God, the creator, have from your earliest years established the appointed course of your life . . . . . .
. . . . I am Nature who, by the gift of my condescension, have made you a sharer in my presence here and have deigned to bless you with my conversation.*

1.

Right-mindedness: a mind in place,
in right relation to Nature and
its neighbors. Thoughts, instructions,
stories, songs enter from outside, and some
of these are needed, can be made welcome,
but nothing replaces the living
geography, topography, ecology, history,
the mind's waking at home in its creaturely
household, which is its work, its burden,
its privilege, its intimate reference, its way
to find at need, against the time's perilous
leanings, the unshifting star.

---

* Alan of Lille (ca. 1116–1202 or 1203), *The Plaint of Nature*, translated by James J. Sheridan, University of Toronto Press, 1980, pp. 117, 126.

2.

In early April a heavy rain
such as never before in my time
scoured the Cane Run watershed,
gathering up everything loose
that the deepening runoff could carry
— mud (the soil!), logs, limbs, old leaves
and weeds, metal containers, bottles, shards
of plastic — the mixed mess left
in drifts on the bottomland pasture.
The land dried, made new and useless
to us by the cumber of the drift.
We picked it up, fourteen loads
of just the pieces big enough to obstruct
the mower, hauled it to the creek,
and threw it in — "If I've learned anything
from physics, it's how to throw things"* —
to be borne away on the ever-continuing
flow.† This was the farm-making,
the lowdown work of the low lands,
never completed as Nature continues
serenely her world-making, in spite
of us if we oppose her, indifferently using us
if we would be her friends. And so
we are brought to her first law
that she, obeying, asks us to obey:
Keep the ground covered, taking *great pains*

---

* My grandson, Marshall Berry, who had finished his first year of college.

† We did not rethrow the metal, glass, and plastic trash into the creek.

35

*. . . to preserve the soil and to prevent
erosion.** Perennial vegetation kept
with care on the uplands and slopes
protects the soil, conserves the rain,
holds in place fertility and provision,
a kindness kept, a kindness given,
granting downstream an unstopping flow.
Good soil is a miracle, at once
holding and letting go. To keep so
kindly the land, the culture aspiring
to be high must cultivate the low
arts of land- and water-keeping.
Nature does not prefer humans
to the fish, the eagles, or the moles.
She *never did betray the heart
that loved her*[†] because she never did
give her preference to any heart,
loving or not. The truth is harder:
If we love ourselves, we have got
to love her. We must study
endlessly her long unending work,
thus learning to do our own, also unending,
making Nature our ally so far
as we can ask and she comply.
"It's good to have Nature working for you,"
said Henry Besuden, who knew.
"She works for a minimum wage."**

---

* Sir Albert Howard, *An Agricultural Testament*, Oxford University Press, 1940, p. 4.

† William Wordsworth, "Lines Composed a Few Miles Above Tintern Abbey."

** See my essay, "A Talent for Necessity," in *The Gift of Good Land*, North Point Press, 1981, p. 231.

3.

Old forest, tall household of the birds, no more
Will nimble deer browse as they did before
Deep in your peaceful shade, and your green mane
No more will gentle summer's sun and rain.

. . . .

All will be mute, Echo be still for good.
There will be a field where your great trees stood,
Their airy shadows shifting in the light. Now
You will feel the coulter and the plow.*

*

From Virginia, they came to wilderness
old past knowing, to them new. A quiet
resided here, into which came these
new ones, minds full of purpose, loud,
small, reductive, prone to disappointment.
They surveyed their places in it, established
possession: *Beginning on the bank*
of the Kentucky River at the mouth of Cane Run
at a hackberry . . .† Within that figment
geography of random landmarks,
the trees were felled. The plows scribed

---

* Pierre de Ronsard (1524–1585), "Lament for the Cutting of the Forest of Gastine," my translation, *A Part*, p. 61. Like Chaucer's and Spenser's, Ronsard's understanding of Nature was reverent, practical, and ecological, as is evident here. This understanding survived in English tradition as far as Pope ("Let Nature never be forgot"). The Romantics forgot the practical connection and the ecological measure.

† From an early "metes and bounds" deed in the history of the locality of these poems.

their lasting passages, exposing the ground
to the sky. The hot sun and hard rain
then came down upon it, undeflected
by a shadow or a leaf. What was here
that they so much wanted to change?
They wanted a farm, not a forest. From then
to now, no caring thought was given
to these slopes ever tending lower.
Thus Nature's gift, her wealth and ours, is borne
downstream, cluttering the bottomlands
in passing, and finally is lost at sea.

*

How with this rage shall beauty hold a plea,
Whose action is no stronger than a flower? *

---

* Shakespeare, Sonnet 65.

4.

It is anno Domini 2014,
the year 239 of the newcomers
into Kentucky, the eightieth year
of the present witness, and now
along the wooded horizons we see
bare ruined tops of the ashes,
beautiful useful trees gone the way
of the landmark elms. This is the work
of the emerald ash borer, another
in the long succession of such articles
of trade — diseases, weeds, noxious
insects, birds, animals, fish —
in the centuries-old global economy:
the side effects, unforeseen
therefore unintended therefore
unknown to those best positioned
to profit by global ignorance therefore
overcharged to Nature, to the land,
to the land communities unknown
as the future to those who take from them
every life and substance transmutable
to money, which fears no plague. And so
in our discounted woods our neighbors
the ash trees suddenly shine
as they die and the woodpeckers
remove the gray outer bark, and we
are poorer on our paltered globe.

5.

What was here that you wanted to change?
You changed at first your absence by your presence,
having arrived by a hard way over
the mountains or along the rivers. Once here,
your presence still was a sort of absence,
for you learned slowly and late where
you were. In ignorance, you destroyed
much that was here that you undervalued,
much of value that you never knew was here.

In ignorance, you have returned again
to absence from this place, this neighborhood
of the living and the dead where for a while
you almost were at home, its names and ways
that for a while were almost on your mind.
What that was here have you given up
for your departure and your absence?
Or if you have stayed, going away
to work, what have you lost, forgetting
where you lay you down to sleep?
Or if you have stayed, driving over the fields
the great machines that have replaced
your neighbors and their work, their laughter
that gave to the work an ancient lightness,
a timeless grace, what have you lost?

Lost in old boundaries now merely
owned or rented at too great a price,
or lost in the dry maps of distances
away, set free of the once-new land
so much desired, so little known,
or tolled away by the old wish

to be as gods, or exiled by decree
of a powerful few against a weak "too many,"*
the people drift in scatters, homeless
as their garbage, on the currents
of a violent economy, their care and work
from their dismemoried country, beyond
every dreamed beginning, lost.

* Soon after World War II the official forces of academic agriculture
and corporate industry determined and declared that there were
"too many farmers." This became government intent, allowing the
"free market" to discount and destroy the small farmers and rural
communities. Too many country people concurred in their own
disvaluation.

6.

A lookout upon a place to work,
live, move, and be in thought
of Nature's ancient precedence and rule,
a small porch from which to see the local
geography as a guide for thinking:

the valley like a cupped hand,
the compassing woods, below the woods
a two-track gravel road, below
the road a low-lying pasture bounded
by a row of trees along a creek,
the creek unseen in its deep slot until,
risen, it spreads upon the ground
the brought-down colors of the sky.

The road is an old way, made
by the wear of coming and going,
rutted by the outwash of storms
breaking across, kept by much
remaking, its life that of humans:
temporal and mortal. Even so,
how beautiful to see the bending
of its two tracks against the falls
and turnings of the slopes. The road divides
woodland and pasture, two ways
of making visible the shifts and passings
of the wind, two ways of giving
voice to the air, two realms of birds.
The invisible finds motion and voice
locally provided. Watch for its signs.

7.

The watcher comes, knowing the small
knowledge of his life in this body
in this place in this world. He comes
to a place of rest where he cannot
mistake himself as larger than he is,
the place of the gray flycatcher,
the yellow butterfly, the green dragonfly,
the white violet, the columbine,
where he cannot mistake himself
as more graced or graceful than he is.

At the woods' edge, the wild rose
is in bloom, beauty and consolation
always in excess of thought.

8.

The pattern for keeping this place
we must take from the woods, if
the land is to thrive in our using.*
If we were not here, Nature
would give this land to trees,
perennial, diverse, conserving
of land and water. The woods
is a great life of many lives
living upon many deaths.
It flourishes in the hidden crypts
of its decay. Seen from anywhere
inside, it is everywhere an unholding
enclosure of many columns,
roofed by the sky, containing
inexhaustibly itself. To the teachable
it is a teaching, not a syllabus
of processes and nomenclature
reduced to human understanding, but
the presence of the world being
made, a fabric of interdepending wonders,
moment by moment completed in beauty,
leaf shadows on light leaves moving.

* *An Agricultural Testament*, pp. 1–4.

9.

To care for what we know requires
care for what we don't, the world's lives
dark in the soil, dark in the dark.

Forbearance is the first care we give
to what we do not know. We live
by lives we don't intend, lives
that exceed our thoughts and needs, outlast
our designs, staying by passing through,
surviving again and again the risky passages
from ice to warmth, dark to light.

Rightness of scale is our second care:
the willingness to think and work
within the limits of our competence
to do no permanent wrong to anything
of permanent worth to the earth's life,
known or unknown, now or ever, never
destroying by knowledge, unknowingly,
what we do not know, so that the world
in its mystery, the known unknown world,
will live and thrive while we live.

And our competence to do no
permanent wrong to the land
is limited by the land's competence
to suffer our ignorance, our errors,
and — provided the scale
is right — to heal, to be made whole.

10.

The conversion of trees to wood to money,
which is all "the economy" asks,
is limitlessly mistakable by arrogance,
for it is the forest, not the trees,
that is the source of economic good:
the forest as the whole community
of itself, its lives living as the gifts
of lives lived. And so we come
to Troy Firth's precaution: Good forestry
is not predetermined by instruction
or methodology handed down by those
who presumably know to those
who presumably don't. It is, above all,
"observational."* Loving the forest,
you enter it to walk and watch.
As you observe its manifold and comely life,
it enters familiarly into imagination,
and so into sympathy. By sympathy
the mind in the forest is made at home.
From knowledge of the forest comes
at last knowledge of forestry:
what, without permanent damage,
can be spared and carefully removed,
leaving the forest whole. This learning
"takes decades. That's all there is to it."[†]

---

* "A Forest Conversation," in my essay collection *Our Only World*,
  Counterpoint, 2015, p. 48.
† "A Forest Conversation," p. 48.

11.

To sit or walk many days
and years, looking from the woods
into the woods, will lead beyond
methodology, beyond even sight,
into the sense, the presence, of the one
life of the forest composed
of uncountable lives in countless
years, each life coherent itself within
the coherence, the great composure,
of all. This no observer could make
or can explain. Within it, every
thought puts the earth at stake.

*

This great Grandmother of all creatures bred
    Great Nature, euer young yet full of eld,
    Still moouing, yet vnmoued from her sted;
    Vnseene of any, yet of all beheld . . .
    . . . .
    To thee O greatest goddesse, onely great,
    An humble suppliant loe, I lowely fly
    Seeking for Right, which I of thee entreat;
    Who Right to all dost deale indifferently...
    . . . .
    Sith of them all thou art the equall mother,
And knittest each to each, as brother vnto brother.*

---

* Edmund Spenser, *The Faerie Queene*, Book VII, Canto VII, stanza
xiii, lines 1–4, and xiv, 1–4, 8–9.

12.

There is nothing random or by-chance (except
when "chance" signifies our ignorance)
in the forming of the woods. The effects
of hard weather, disease, human carelessness,
even these are caught up like dropped stitches,
gathered into the whole fabric, carried from
what was to what is to what will be. This is
the forest native to this place, its form
ever complete, never ending, grace beyond
all human comprehending. This is the form
of causes leading to effects that in turn
become causes, "the boundary of causation
always exceeding the boundary of consideration,"
as Wes Jackson puts it.* The form is shown
first by the shapes of leaves repeating,
like the chorus of a song. Trunk and branches
from the dark rise, divide, taper out and out,
each tree recalling a form never perfectly embodied
that yet is recognizable by kind among the mix
of kinds and their crisscrossings, each shaped
according to kind and company, place
and time, each by its story made among
the stories of the others. Each form is made
by reaching among shadows for light. It is shaped
by circumstances that its shaping changes.

* Often, in conversation.

13.

Explainers speak of the "stratification" of the forest: the tops of the tallest trees are "the canopy," then comes "the understory" of smaller trees, below those is "the shrub layer" of tallish woody bushes that are not trees, below those is "the herb layer" of ferns and flowers. Of all the strata above the ground the lowest is "the litter layer" of dead and decaying leaves, tree-fragments, fallen trees.*

These terms are useful, even true. And yet the forest does not stand still to be thus diagrammed. The tallest trees are found, at various ages, in every layer — to speak of one additional complexity. And yet all of the forest's parts, named or unnamed, known or unknown, are the forest.

We must include also the ferns, the fungi, mosses, lichens, vines, the creatures willfully mobile who crawl, walk, run, climb, glide, and fly, who pose to be pictured, described, and studied most readily when dead, whose needs and purposes, moods and motions all are contained, never extraneous or strange, within the ever-forming form.

* John Kricher / Gordon Morrison, *A Field Guide to Ecology of Eastern Forests*, The Peterson Field Guide Series, p. 7. (In fact, despite my quibble here, a pleasing, useful, recommendable book.)

14.

Birds people the heights, the low flyways,
the hidden passages among flowers and ferns.
And many times the watcher has imagined
what he may know but never see: the brooding vireo
in a thunderstorm at night, calmly roofing
her nest with her body and her wings while in
the dark the whole tree bends, the slender
branch stoops and swings, the hard rain falls.

15.

There is never an end to imagining
the lives of the birds. Or to wondering
at the superfluous beauty and unspeaking
flight of butterflies who light nearby:
the Eyed Brown, the Spicebush Swallowtail,
the Red Admiral, the Red-spotted Purple.
These so visible must stand for countless ones
and kinds easily overlooked or hard to see
or invisible. A world of words could not
describe this wordless world.

16.

The above-ground woods is fortified,
sustained, immeasurably is made,
by the half of it that is underground.
We must acknowledge first that it is dark,
and we are blind by sight. This is the stratum
known only by result, where the dead become
alive, where the seed, abiding alone, dies
into the commonwealth of the living. We see
only by the light we bring, never to know
the dark lives as they are lived
in the dark. We mine out of this darkness,
according to our light, facts as dry
as bones. Can these facts live?

*

And in a launde, upon an hil of floures,
Was set this noble godesse Nature.
Of braunches were here halles and here boures
Iwrought after here cast and here mesure . . .
. . . .
Nature, the vicaire of the almyghty Lord . . .*

* Chaucer, *The Parliament of Fowles*, lines 302–5, 379.

17.

The woods in beauty is made complete,
leaf shadows on light leaves moving
with the motions of the air.

So is the lowly pasture completed
in beauty, the bergamot, the milkweed
declaring themselves in season
among the ripened grass stems,
the grassblades, the blossoming clovers.

But are these beautiful because
we think them so, or because they are
beautiful in the mind of Nature
or the mind of God, beautiful
by intention inborn in a world beloved?

Beauty is the crisis of our knowing,
the signature of love indwelling
in all created things, called from nothing
by love, recognized and answered
by love in the human heart, not reducible
by any analysis to any fact.

The sufficient fact is unavailable.
The creatures came, as love imagines,
answering the loneliness of God
who needed them for company, as we
in our loneliness have needed them.

18.

Love is the crisis of our work.
When the watcher speaks of love
he is speaking not of history, not
of past or future, but of the love
in which all time has moved, in which
all things were and are and are to be,
the love that is before the beginning,
 that is beyond the end, that is
entirely present as the flower of a day.

19.

Thus kan I forme and peynte a creature,
Whan that me list; who kan me countrefete?

. . . .

For He that is the formere principal
Hath maked me his vicaire general,
To forme and peynten erthely creaturis
Right as me list, and ech thyng in my cure is
Under the moone, that may wane and waxe;
And for my werk right no thyng wol I axe;
My lord and I been ful of oon accord
I made hire to the worshipe of my lord . . .*

*

Rising out of the crowd of lowly
foliage on the woods floor, a few
days in June, the white penstemon
risks the distinction of bloom.
At the top of the slender stem
the cluster of flowers appears,
not surprising for it is known
from other years, but as if suddenly
returned. Each tubular blossom,
pure white, five-lobed, opens
to reveal in its throat seven stripes
of most delicate purple, the middle stripe
the longest, with three shorter ones
symmetrically spaced on either side.

. . .

* Chaucer, *The Physician's Tale*, lines 11–13, 19–26.

For this, flower and watcher have not
waited or prepared, but merely lived
and the time of bloom has come.
For whose delight? The watcher gives
his sole certainty: "For mine." And what
depends upon this small culmination?
An ecologist of sorts, the watcher
does not know, but by its beauty
he is taught to answer: "Everything."

This is the Sabbath, the place, the rest,
from which we go to work. From here
the economies and politics of husbandry
are quietly attested in the heart.

20.

The forest serves the human economy merely by being a forest, giving to our use what we call its "products" and, if rightly used and spared, remaining a forest, intact, diversely living, after the gift is made. The pasture, like the forest, is Nature's gift, answerable to her laws. Like the well-kept woodland, the pasture, well-kept, covers and secures the soil, gentles and conserves the rain.

Unlike the forest, the pasture depends for its existence upon the farmer, his purpose, and his work. It is thus also a human artifact, maintained by grazing or mowing or both to interrupt the succession of plants by which the forest would return.

Because the farmer has made and kept it by his effort, his care for the grasses, clovers, weedy forages, and for the animals that live by grazing, his love for the pasture is unlike his love for the woods, but not greater.

The difference is made by his delight
in the delight, the fulfilled hunger,
of the good beasts of his choosing,
who depend on him, on whom
he depends. And all depends upon
a knowing, workday loving
to guide him in his work and watching.

21.

He wants to see the pasture green and thriving, satisfying the hunger of his sheep, who graze their fill, drink their fill at the creekside, lie down in the shade to rest. In their rest rests the shepherd's soul.

The pasture joins its keepers to the world by ties, human and natural, more complex than they know, or will ever know. It keeps the harmony between economy and nature without which in human care neither can thrive.

It is economic by its yield of yearly life to the farm and its household. Subject only to human care and keeping, it is natural in its lasting, in its feeding of animals that feed people, in its living upon its own dying year after year, in its own community of creatures by humans uninvited.

The pasture joins its health
to the farmer's pleasure by the thriving
of his flock as it grazes among
the self-invited flowers,
by the nests the ground-nesting birds
have studiously placed and hidden,
by the covert nests and passages
of mice and voles, by the flights
of dragonflies, butterflies, fireflies,
by the delighted swallows flying.

22.

When the ground is safely kept,
when the scale is right, and when
the resident human mind
is righted by memory, affection,
neighborly kindness and care,
the giving of hands to work,
all the lives of woodland and pasture
live by the economy of gifts,
the only economy that will last.
To be in one's right mind
is to know the right use of gifts.
To ask for more than is given,
to take more than is given back,
is to have less, and finally
nothing. This is not because
of any human wish. It follows
the law of Nature, mother
of all the creatures, maker
and giver of the native patterns
by which our world in changing
lasts, in dying lives.

*

Imposter, do not charge most innocent Nature,
As if she would her children should be riotous
With her abundance; she, good cateress,
Means her provision only to the good,
That live according to her sober laws
And holy dictate of spare Temperance.*

* John Milton, *Comus*, lines 762–67.

23.

Life does not relent or become
easier as death approaches
and troubles accumulate with age.
To pray to keep your mind as made
is as fearful as to pray to live,
for you may live into knowledge
worse than death. To forget
that some knowledge can be worse
than death is to be worse than dead.
How then may you come yet alive
to right-mindedness and right prayer?
Rightness of mind is only to be at home
in the place and the life you were given.
Rightness of prayer is only this:
Teach me thy love to know;
That this new light, which now I see,
*May both the work and workman show . . .**

* George Herbert, "Mattens."

24.

Almost lost in the mass
of neighboring foliage,
a plant clumsily named
Green-stemmed Joe-pye Weed
is singled out finally
by a cluster of pale blossoms.
It is not the most notable
of flowers, and yet once
an afternoon the sunlight
finds a way through
a hundred feet of leaves
and for a moment the shy
Green-stemmed Joe-pye Weed
receives that light and shines
in answer. Happy the man
who then is watching.

IX.

1.

The expert on resistance to torture
becomes an expert torturer.
The machine that helped a woman
to do her work replaces her at work.
The machine that helped a man to think
ticks on in absence of the man.
The communications technology that was
to become the concourse and meeting
of all the world, bringing the longed-for
peace to all the world, becomes
a weapon to break the world in pieces.

2.

Surely there is simple wrong, wrong
from the start, but the turning wrong
is worse: gains containing the seeds
of loss, amenities fated to do harm.
To warm our houses we set the world afire.
The gullible, the frivolous, the hard of heart
make of modern miracles normal
terror and perpetual war.
The first robot we heard of was a bomb.

3.

Will the robotic tree perform
the original miracle, transforming
light into life? Will the robotic leader
come at last to achieve our objective,
feed the hungry, forgive the debtors,
heal the sick, give sight to the blind,
release the captives, raise the dead?
Or do we look for another?

4.

If we surely knew that the man before us,
single in the multitude, would wreck
the plane that would wreck the tower,
whose fall would wreck a multitude,
who would not kill him?
If we knew for certain that the one man
in the cell would, if tortured, tell
the truth and save a multitude,
who would not torture him?

5.

After the mathematic of the Crucifixion,
who would not destroy one to save
a multitude, if by the destruction of one
so many reliably could be saved?
But that is as numbers are, and of us
who can foretell the future of numbers?
One small seed, lost in the multitude,
dying in the ground, sends into light
a mighty tree. But that is the original miracle
returned once again in time, and who of us
can foretell in time the future of a miracle?

6.

As the future is to fear, the ones gather
into the many who must be killed
unendingly, at endless expenditure
of death for life, of money for death,
of weapons for money. And the economy
grows unendingly, a faith to borrow
unendingly against, as the future is to fear.

7.

And we who walk in darkness,
the darkness we call our day, lighted
by the burning world, we need
the darkness for the foretold salvation:
We will save humanity by our willingness
to become inhuman. To save the world
we await the beneficent machine.

8.

O hasten, hasten through the dark
under the dim reminding stars
to find again what is small, tender, beloved,
the hope and mercy of this world
at the mercy of this world
in the darkest dark, the longest night.

9.

When our first grandchild came
to be with us, my father held back, unable
to bring himself again to give his heart
to another child, another who would
call forth his love, no matter the cost.
And then, knowing her smallness, her helplessness,
her inheritance of this world's sorrow,
he gave his heart, and so was given
what he had suffered longest and needed most.

2015

I.

In the stiffened air the country hardens
into black and white, trees and snow.
Nothing moves but us warm-blooded ones
who walk and fly. In sky and river only
the living stir. My heart's fellow birds
come to the feeders for the seeds of their lives.
In our old world we live and wait
for the waters to flow, the winds to blow.

II.

You can divide a bird from its life,
your blade passing perfectly between.
But what you have then is not a life
and a bird. You have a dead bird
whose life now is nowhere you know.
After the passage of the blade, your study
of life has become the study of death.
Life cannot be stopped, its particles
divided and studied. Though life is
the part of a creature that causes it
to live, it seems in itself not a part
but rather a whole in which parts
of the world for a while participate.

III.

Nightmares of the age invade
my days and darken them,
but sometimes my sleep is lighted
by a better dream. One night,
as if in justice perhaps or mercy,
or by some kindness of this world,
I dreamed of my father. Long ago
he would play the piano, lively songs
of World War II, rocking on the bench,
sometimes singing, as he played.
And then a lasting sorrow came,
and no more piano music after that.
In my dream my father was again
playing the piano. He was beautiful.
He was smiling. He was playing
an elated improvisation on a tune
neither of us had known in the old time.
The notes shone singly as they gathered
brightly together. "Daddy," I said,
"you could play anywhere!" He smiled
at his thought's music, and played on.

IV.

We sleep and wake, wake
and sleep within the surrounding
sound of the falling rain,
hard at times, and the thunder,
all night long.

We don't need nearly so much
but so much is what we get,
no use complaining
or explaining: "It is climate change."
It is the climate.

The climate of this spring
will bring the woods' wildflowers
into bloom pretty much
together, glorious
all those old little ones
by the late cold and snow delayed,
by too much rain brought on,

who so far keep returning,
who have survived so far
the worst the climate can do,
and will this year survive
the present bad also.

What will be hurt by this
too much, and often much less,
will be the naked fields,
thoughtlessly used, and then
absent from thought.

.   .   .

The earth thus regardlessly
is dispersed abroad, never
to return, not when
better thought may wish it back.

V.

They believe they've understood
belief in "the transcendent"
by disbelieving it.

Some mental feats remain
impossible even to the best
of human minds.

VI.

Now comes the overflow
not to be imagined but in time,
in season, in presence. This is
the splurge of beauty, transcending
every need we know. In her
greater knowing, great dame Nature
has called them, and they come,
the flowers in their thousands
under the still-bare trees, over
the dead leaves rising, moving
lightly as the air moves:
twinleaf, bloodroot, anemone,
violets purple and yellow and white,
bellwort. And the bluebells, whose perfume
cannot be recalled until
they are called back again. Who
would refuse this joy, this gift,
because in time it cannot last?

VII.

What a wonder I was
when I was young, as I learn
by the stern privilege
of being old: how regardlessly
I stepped the rough pathways
of the hillside woods,
treaded hardly thinking
the tumbled stairways
of the steep streams, and worked
unaching hard days
thoughtful only of the work,
the passing light, the heat, the cool
water I gladly drank.

VIII.

Love is a universe beyond
The daylight spending zone:
As one we more abound
Than two alone.

IX.

And now this holding
has held fifty-eight years,
a larger life we've lived in,
a welcoming room, a window
opening to the world.

5/29/15

X.

"Patriotism" blasts and crackles
all over the distant sky
while, blinking their silent code,
the fireflies rise out of the grass.

But wait. Call them "lightening bugs"
as we've always called them here.
Called by their right name,
they lighten our minds.

7/4/15

XI.

He sees by the light of the sun
and the sky's other lights
that come and go, revealing
at each return the changes
of the world, and the changes made
by humans of the world in time
for better or worse, some fearfully
for the worse. He sees also
by light given by teachers and friends
and the light that is left behind
in pictures, stories, and songs,
a staying light made
of the light's passing. As a further
wonder he has learned
to see by a light inborn
in himself, as in every leaf.
At last it has come to him
by being with him all along.
Of the world's one light, these
are the parcels he has gathered,
making a smaller light, his
by his willing to see by it.

To that light, itself invisible
were it not for the world
that is lighted by it, comes spring,
the circumstance of leaves,
the leaflight changing as the leaves
move, a motional language
of the invisible air, in which
also the colors of the flowers
declare the flowers amid

the crowding green leaves.
To see that these are wonders
he has only to wonder.
By loving them he sees
in them the signature
of the shaping love inwardly
moving them to bloom, as the air
moves them outwardly.

The machine that measures the light
does not see it. He sees
over the summer pasture
the dark swallowtails among
the beebalm's lavender flowers,
beauty far beyond
any purpose that he knows.
Beyond any hope
he could have had, he sees
among the shadows by the creek
the blue bellflowers suddenly
blooming on their frail towers.
The world lives by its beauty
in excess of need. In excess
of his absence, he is here
in the Sabbath beyond his reasons,
the Sabbath of measureless delight.

XII.

The old man is in the last days
of work he has done and loved
for many years. He is mowing
with his old team, the white horse
and the black, on the open hillside
under the open sky, within
the surrounding woods. This work
once was known by many
of his kind, and he is one
of the last to know it. But now
as his time grows scarce, his work
rarer by the day, its sights and motions
could be filmed, its sounds recorded,
it could be preserved perhaps forever
by wonders of modern technology.
He says no. He thinks no.
He refuses with his whole heart
the already futile wish to make
of a past present a future past.
Being so saved, his days
would be lost, would be no longer
even a memory. He needs these last
of his workdays. He needs them to be
his last, his own, such days
as do not come to one unwilling
to let them go. Had he been unwilling
for them to go, they would not yet
have come. Had he not been glad
to be the only one to know them,
he would never have known them.
If he remembers them to the last, giving
his thanks, how great will be his reward!

XIII.

The best of human work defers
always to the in-forming beauty
of Nature's work. But human work,
true to the nature of places
as it should be, is not natural
and is not a mirror held up
to nature. At best it is
the gift of the Heavenly Muse
to the farmer's art or the poet's,
by endless learning learned,
forever incomplete.

It is only the Christ-life,
the life undying, given,
received, again given,
that completes our work.

XIV.

1.

The creek in flood at night
is the auger that bores the hole
in time, through which we see
the making of the world, the water
loosed, floating the big rocks
beating them together, the rocks
beating the trees, the order
of the flow overcoming the order
of the staying ground, tearing it,
melting it, carrying it away.

2.

Our very fields are flowing,
earth burdening the waters.
To be made thus new,
the place must be made less.
And we who walk upon it
as it is being made
submit ourselves to making
by it as we have made it,
its history and ours made
day by day the same.

3.

How sweetly at other times
the flow declines, moving
silently from the riffle above
to the riffle below, the still
surface bearing fallen leaves
dry upon it, and as slow
as clouds in the bluest sky.

XV.

Again the air is full
of falling: the fall of the leaves
in the weighty season that brings
all home again to the lowly
miracle from which they came.

Nature, the mother and maker,
requires that life take form,
enflesh itself in the shapes
and habits of the world's unnumbered
kinds. And then she requires
each one at last to shed
its guise, giving up
its matter to the life to come.

Think of a world of no fall,
no gravity calling downward,
homeward, bringing all
by the light uprisen down
to rest in the resting land
— a world, instead, where all
that dies would fly upward
and outward, nameless and alone.
How sterile then would be
the earth, seasonless the year.

The year is the showing forth
of the heavenly love that is
the being of the present world.
The leaves, opening and at last
falling, hold a while
the beauty of God who made them

by the work and care of Nature,
His vicar and our mother.
His only is the light
of which all things are made,
the beauty that they are,
the delight that is our prayer.

XVI.

The year falls also from
the human-borne plagues
that kill the trees, foul
the air, the water, and the earth,
bringing to the world the curse
of frivolous death, the tiresome
novelty of wastefulness,
the ugly forethoughtfulness of fear.

What repair, what
return, will undo the consuming
self-belittlement that inherits,
disvalues, neglects, and ruins
the decent small farm —
the earned, kept, and cherished
good of a lifetime's work
gone — to break the heart?

And yet the light comes.
And yet the light is here.
Over the long shadows
the late light moves
in beauty through the living woods.

✿❀✿❀✿❀✿❀✿❀ 2016 ✿❀✿❀✿❀✿❀✿❀

I.

One white anemone,
the year's first flower,
saves the world.

II.

Across the distance he saw
his granddaughter arriving
at a meeting he was leaving.

They called to each other
in greeting and farewell.
"I love you, Granddaddy."

"I love you too, honey,"
he called back, and it was
his father's voice he heard

uttered as his own, as from
the distance behind him.
And so he remembered

again the ancient lineage
of his love, given to him
and again given, living

backward, time beyond
time, to the Love that called
to itself the heaven and the earth.

III.

How I wish I could have been
already a young man
already waiting for you
the day you were born, and then
I could have been already
almost your husband, loving you
from your first birthday, as
in fact I do, beautiful as I knew you
always, and I waiting
while you grew to womanhood
to recognize me then
as your husband first and last,
and our life together could begin.

4/30/16

IV.

When I speak to you of love
I do not speak as I am
but as I am in love with you
which is better than I am.

5/29/16

V.

For his while remaining, he
would like to liken himself
to the shadowy flycatcher,
the watcher, on his dead branch
at the clearing's edge, standing
ready to fly, his eye ever alert
to the now that has ever been.

VI.

The watcher has come, as quiet
as a shade, into the shadow
of the ever-stirring woods.
The small bird he loves
who likes his porch, his narrow
clearing, comes near him
and is not afraid, at ease
in the overlap between
her mindfulness and his.
For a time the pair of them
equally find nothing to say,
their quiet a kindly speech
mutually understood.

VII.

What might not a poet write
if the beautiful orange fritillary
Aphrodite should light
more than a moment on his hand.

VIII.

WHAT PASSES, WHAT REMAINS

Here the mingling of the waters
of Shade Branch, Sand Ripple,
the dishonored Kentucky River,
tells the history of our country
which is the history of our people.
Here the mind submits
itself to be shaped, and so
it shapes its thought, partly
of itself, partly of all
in time it has come to know.
Here in this passage of valley
hollowed by the passage of water,
great Life has come in passing
to inhabit every body
inhabiting this place,
giving desire and motion,
giving sight, light,
color, and form, giving
stories, songs, calls,
cries, outcries. How long?

This is the place in which
the living live in the absence
of all who once were here,
their stories kept a while
in memories soon to be gone
the way of the untongued stories

preceding ours, reduced
to graves mostly lost
and a few found strayed
artifacts of stone.

Of those now living here
already few recall
the names of the Rowanberrys
whose home this rough land was
that bears in presence only
their worn ways, some scars
their work made, the well
the early ones dug and walled
where their log house stood
and burned, the disassembled
chimneys, the sundered hearths.
Their numberless disappeared
footsteps are traceable now
only by the remaining few
who remember the last of them.

By love we keep them with us,
and so we have remembered
ourselves as members, gathered
in Love's household that stands
surpassingly in time: we few
remaining, who keep the stories.

"My lord, they worked hard
for every nickel and dime
they ever had. One crop

finished and gone to market,
they'd start clearing a patch
of hillside for the next crop.
If you look about, you'll find
their monuments that will last, I reckon,
clean to Judgment Day:
big piles or squared cairns
of rocks turned up by their plows,
dragged out of the furrows,
lifted and put down, and nothing
automatic into it, neither.
Here and there you'll find
their gullies too, mostly healed
under the young woods about
the age of an old man."

"I was grubbing bushes
and sprouts with an axe, setting
my own pace, but hard at it.
Art and Mart were felling
and logging up the trees
with a two-man crosscut saw.
After a while Mart said, 'Pascal,
I'll rest you a little. Let me
run that axe, and you
get here on the saw with Art.'
So we traded, and good God!
I felt like I had a hold
of the tail of a stout big calf
and couldn't turn loose. Even
what they called rest was *work*.
And Mr. Early Rowanberry
—the old man, but not so old

then as I thought—he
would be working always, always
somewhere ahead of them."

"He come in there at Burgess's
one evening late, a bunch
of us loafing there, talking,
the way we'd do. He bought
a steel-beam rounder plow,
paid in cash, and then
did what not a one of us
foresaw. He'd come walking.
It was a *heavy* plow. Somebody
would have hauled it down there
for him in a day or two.
He picked it up by the beam of it
and laid it over his shoulder
like it wasn't more than a hoe,
hunched it into place,
and set off home on the path
down Shade Branch, a mile
to walk and it getting dark.
Lord amighty! Hurrying
to be ready to work in the morning,
I reckon. No time to lose."

"Oh, it hurts me to remember
how hard my daddy worked."

And she by then was old
after a life of her own
hard work, hers and Pascal's,
by which they bought, paid for,

and improved their farm, built
and paid for a good small house.
Theirs had been a time
kinder to them than her father's
had been to him. Their life
even so had been in its way
a triumph of work and thrift,
care and self-respect.
Whoever knew them knew
something inarguably good.

"A while after we got married
and set up housekeeping
over across the river,
knowing she missed her folks,
I brought Sudie back home
for a visit late that winter.
It sleeted during the night.
In the morning all outdoors
was coated with ice. They'd been
cleaning up another
hillside for another crop:
felling the trees, grubbing
out the bushes, closing in
on a great big snarl of briars
still in the way. After
breakfast, Mr. Rowanberry
sent us boys to the barn,
slipping and sliding on the ice,
to do the chores. And he
took down his scythe from its nail
and went to the hillside to mow
that big blackberry patch
before the day warmed up

and melted off the ice
from the catclaws of the briars."

And so some days they were favored,
when place and work and weather
seemed to answer one another,
when what the world asked
and what they gave seemed
almost in rhyme, hour
after hour, daylight to dark,

days too when the world asked
for all they had to give
and more, when a boy, under
the demand of a father, brittled
and driven, could wish to be
some place he could not go.

"My daddy remembered Art Rowanberry
disking ground with a team of mules
when he wasn't more than eight years old.
His feet didn't reach to the frame of the harrow,
and his daddy had tied him onto the seat
with a little piece of cotton rope.
He was all the help his daddy had.
I don't reckon Art remembered
when he didn't know how to drive a team."

"Art enlisted in the army in '42
when he was thirty-seven years old.
In basic training he rested up.
He said he gained a little weight."

. . .

"To stand around waiting to work,
that was something I had to *learn*.
One day they give us out some axes,
thick as your foot, dull as a froe.
I taken a file and whetted mine
to where it was some account. Them boys
just stood around and watched me chop."

"He was the oldest, the eldest son.
He thought if he went, the younger ones
would be spared. But they drafted two of them.
If he hadn't enlisted, Art might not
have had to go. But oh my!
He saw a world he'd never dreamed of,
and dreamed of, I reckon, the rest of his life."

"I stopped in Bastogne with a buddy of mine
and we bought us a big plate of potatoes.
We still were eating them when the Germans
cut us off. Before that was done with
we *needed* a big plate of potatoes.
We was hungry, down to just
one little pancake a day."

I said, "I reckon you all were glad
when they broke through and got you out."
And he said, seeming to look and see it
again through almost forty years,
"We was glad to see that day when it come."

"It was during the war, I reckon.
I don't remember why,
but I was mowing weeds
with an old machine we had

and my good team of mules.
The weeds was tall as the mules
and it was smothering hot,
punishing hot, the air
flying full of chaff
and biting flies. And that
old leftover machine,
you had to run it fast
to make it cut at all.
I hit a stump and broke
the cutter bar clean off.
I never was as glad
of anything in my life"
—Mart.

　　　Or any of them,
at work in the hot sun,
might have looked into the woods
at the trees standing in shade
at ease and quiet, and thought
again that man must earn
his bread by the sweat of his face.

Mart, who here stands
imperfect as he knew he was,
was rightly somewhat glad
that when the Reckoning came
and he stood before his Maker
he would at least have met
the terms of our condition, discharged
his debt, his account of sweat
and labor paid in full.

.　.　.

At last, when we'd worked together,
through the morning, and Flora
asked, as we came into the kitchen
for dinner, glad to see him
as she always was, "How're you,
Art?" Art said, "Well,
they say you're once a man
and twice a child, and I believe
I've been through just about
all them possibilities."

Now they and all their days
are gone into the silence
and invisibility that come
with an old man's gathered years
to hover over the home,
the known, land. None
like them will ever live
in such a time as theirs
in such a place as this
place was in their time.

Eternal in its passing, Life
came to them, offering its gifts,
making its demands, and they
answered by their work, their pleasure,
their enduring, knowing at times
a timelessness in which
they woke as living souls.

To one who has watched and remembered,
listened and remembered, in time
sharing the work and the weather,
the laughter and the grief, it seems

that Life is with us always
as a wide wind passing
through the woods, moving
every leaf. As it gives us
our lives and then, as we
have made them, takes them away,
a fitting care remains
as ever still and whole
in our great Taskmaster's eye.

IX.

The old man in his latter days
prays his thanks, prays his love
of the world to the world's end,
for out of the perils of his faith,
of human wrongs, of his own mistakes,
he has recovered the thought,
the memory almost, so close
to him it seems, of the man
not of this world, born of this world,
who came to a place on the hillside
and, seeing the multitude, sat down
and into the quiet quietly blessed,
all the sufferers, all the troubled ones.

X.

If not for mortality and its troubles
all humans would be idiots or
monsters, for they would see no limits
to their selves and their hungers. This
declares the dependence of our kindness
upon the future, of which we know
nothing but that our limits will be met.

XI.

The Sabbath of the standing woods
is our refuge from our age's will,
its machines and poisons, noises
and fires. It is the Sabbath
of will-less receiving and our thanks.

XII.

Sleep undefended in the dark
entrusted to the light that so far
has waked you to the morning
that (whatever the news) is singing.

XIII.

The hidden bird is singing
"All right. Yes. Yes yes. All right."

Nothing worth saying
ever is finally said.

2017

I.

Now I remember the times you have drawn me forth
out of singleness and the perishing day,
when I again became the bridegroom, you the bride,
and we answered an imperative we did not make
in a world no mortal hands had made,
a world that was another world.

And now I remember the hasty grave
in the garden at dawn on the third day,
the woman in despair coming early to find
that clovers opened, all alright,
as I know by love, if I know anything.

4/30/17

II.

The lamb, newborn, has come
with strength to stand and suck.
Its first sucking gives
strength to suck again,
and so again, and so
it lives. All the living world
tends toward this can-be
so ordinary, frail, and necessary:
through all chance and change,
all failing, this constancy.

III.

The animate lily
prefers as I do
light and warmth
to dark and cold,
and so it opens
in the morning early,
so at last it closes
as the dark rises and
comes down. So we agree
and are at peace
in our neighborhood.

IV.

IN THE THICKET

God's Truth as God knows it

as it can be told in a human tongue

as it can survive translation from one tongue to another

as it can survive interpretation by scholars

as it can survive the teachings of teachers

as it can survive in the experience, understanding, and
     language of every human

as it is—visible to those who see—still in the made
     world beautiful

as it partly may be restored by good sense, lovingkindness, and
     good will, by inspiration, by beautiful work.

V.

Slow, here by the river,
is the story of the growth of trees
and their replacement by younger trees.

Slower is the story of the swaying
of the river in its bends
against the valley sides, a movement
long in time made
by swiftness of risen water.

Quick and final is the story
of the man sitting and watching
on the shore, the sun burning,
the leaves stirring, the birds
singing by the flowing water.

VI.

As the flock enters the fold
for the night, the young ewe comes
with them, but she is calling
her lamb, her only, who is not
with her. Calling, she hurries
back to the pasture, and I
with her. Her lamb looks,
as the dead sometimes do,
almost alive. I carry it
and the ewe follows, calling,
and so we grieve. We're two
of a kind, calling in the dark
in the dark.

VII.

How could we have known?
In choosing each other
we chose unknowing our story,
all these years, here
by the river, all these people
who came as strangers, belonging
to this love that long ago
we entered and remained.

5/29/17

VIII.

For Carol Besse

You have seen many birds,
some commonly known, some rare.
But, like me, you know
that the rarest and most fair
is the one that could have been
any one, the one unknown,
from the quivering branch
just flown. But once I saw,
hardly looking, without expecting,
the brightest tanager from the top
of the tallest tree to something
delectable on the ground drop
straight as a falling star.

IX.

"O dark, dark, dark, amid the blaze of noon . . ."
                    —*Samson Agonistes*

There was a time when people
of the light of ordinary day
saw also by the Heavenly light
that now to us is dark.
They witnessed as ordinarily real
creatures and events that to us
are unreal. And so we no longer
see that long ago there was
a land by Heaven favored
with forests and meadows, everlasting
springs, everflowing streams, all
alive with the health
that is wholeness that is holiness.
And to that land came
a people like ourselves
who made it all their own.
They so much desired
all they thought it was
they destroyed it for its wealth
that they possessed only
by spending and by burning.

X.

The world thrives as God's gift
within gratitude. Thanklessness
consumes it: a muddy stream
washing the beautiful field away.

XI.

After many meetings, much talk,
return to the company of trees,
the luxury of wordlessness,
unsounding needlessness,
the great silence that speaks
for itself, until in answer
a living word may come,
lighting on the opened page.

XIII.

All around, the tall trees
unmoving in the ground,
agile in the breeze.

XIII.

If you put your mind to it,
if you quit explaining
everything by naming
its parts, then you know
a great tenderness in the lives
of living creatures. You see it
least and most in the flowering
of our commonest aster, millions
of its white, yellow-centered
least of flowers perfected
in the least of buds, a making
great in its smallness,
delicate beyond touch
of light or sight, through many
ages, many days.

XIV.

The long night comes and Christ is slain
And yet we glimpse His birth again,
Amid the high magnificence
Of our self-praise and self-defense,
Reduced now to the original scale
Of an actual manger, an actual stall.

The heavenly light of a kindly star
Obscured by veils of wealth and power
Was bright to shepherds who left their fold
To see the humblement foretold:
Immortal Word in a mortal child
In the mortal world then less defiled

Than now. But still by halo light
We see the new-fleshed Word—so slight
A quickening, a kindled splinter
In a cold house in the dead of winter.
Small as it was and may remain,
It is complete as falling rain.

✿❀✿❀✿❀✿❀✿❀✿ **2018** ✿❀✿❀✿❀✿❀✿❀✿

I.

The phoebes dance
in the air, on the branch,
their love for one another.

Their tails' flair,
their wings in the air
announce this will go further.

II.

That you were born in April
is again a happy thing.
After so many years
the woods wild flowers still
light, and the birds still sing.
The old dog lies in the sun
out of the wind, dreams
and is warm. So it is
with me because you were born.

4/30/18

III.

My reputation for deploring harm
seems to be improving.
I sit on the porch with my book,
moved but unmoving,
and a wren comes feeding
within reach of my arm.
In courtesy, I look,
look away, and keep reading.

IV.

Long memory dares me on this day
to recall the half-a-boy I was
sixty-one years ago, fallen
in love with you. Yes, that tattered
cliché is true. Shot from a blind,
I had will-lessly fallen from all
I had so far thoughtlessly been
into the beginning of what I would
be becoming from then on, never
entirely ready to receive
the gift you had been, and were, and would be
always somewhat to my surprise.
I'm being humble to keep true
to this life remaining yours and mine
and ours, this wonder I will need
sixty-one more years at least
to live up to. To begin, then, this
poem wishing to be a gift.

5/29/18

V.

My fathers commended to me
with passion when I was young
the teamster who sat straight up,
alert, when he worked his team.
This was our cosmos when I was young.
A good mule was a lesson to me.
So was the cow who gave most cream
and the eagerest setter pup
and the cat that covered its dung.

VI.

Art Rowanberry, indignant

Something better, something better!
Everybody's talking about something better!
The important thing is to feel good
and be proud of what you *got*, don't matter
if it ain't nothing but a log pen!

VII.

Late August, and the leaves
start to fall, set free
by their little weight in the still
air and the light still green
in the lofts and steeps of the trees.

VIII.

May be the soul hereafter suffers
all its shames once more
to pay for them in kind, and then,
its fines finally paid, is free
to delight perfectly at last
in all its old delights.

IX.

1.

"Well, it's a fascinating world,"
my friend said, "after all,"
"after all" meaning he was ill,
standing on the world's edge,
and he knew he was. He was and is
my teacher, one of us who gathered
here, wearing flesh in our time,
to work together, to sweat and laugh,
to love one another. And I am
senior to him now by thirty years.

I am living at last into
the solitude of which my mother
spoke: Who, with whom she had lived
in her place and time, could she ask now
to remind her of what she had forgot?
It is no privilege to become the one
living authority on your life.

2.

The joy of swallow flight again
is gone from the sky, and the old sorrow
of the passing year returns. A greater
sorrow is to love the good now lost
by our ancient flaw made worse.
The rain falls on the fields left bare,
the earth melts and flows away.
And now we pay our wages in remorse,
having made a gift the means of loss.

The rain returns. The land once gone,
like time and life and the dead, stays gone.
It is no distinction to have seen the last
of much good gone forever.
But men and women have lived here
in this bad time and times before
whose names brighten the thought of heaven.

And from her window Tanya saw
the ironweeds dancing in the rain.

3.

After the sorrows that come in the night,
though he is old and weary, the worker,
the watcher of the fields and woods, wakes
in the morning, his right work before him
waiting to be done. He does it, in doing it
is happy, not waiting for praise or asking
for hope. The day passes and the light
prints his shadow on the ground.

And the faithful world offers still
its fascination, after all. In the cold
come the bluebirds, a small bright flock
too lively to count. By wearing through winter
his dull coat, the goldfinch comes
shining into spring. Having been here
all along, the wild rose is revealed
in bloom beside the daily road.
The lambs penned, fed, and all right,
the shepherd, comforted, goes home for the night.

Up, Lord, and let not man have the upper hand . . .

Psalm 9:19 (Coverdale)

I.

An act of kindness is not
an advance, not progress,
but only a triumph. The unfound
organ we call "the heart"
has survived another day.

II.

Our old Maggie too
came at last to the great edge
and kept on going.

III.

1.

In the dark of night, the whole dark
from the bedrock and within it
to the farthest sky, the roots wake
and stir. Life begins its venture
upward to the passing day,
remembering the forms and colors
of the little flowers that come first
to the cold woods. And a time was,
once in time, when you, like them astir
in the dark, were coming to the light
as I before you had come, given form
by the hand that works first
in the dark, the dark that waited
for us to meet in it and know
ourselves by the joining of our hands.

4/30/19

2.

And we go on, my old love,
as before into the dark,
leaving behind us errors and losses
enough, while also we gathered
gifts from each other, from others,
from this dear place and our life
made here by our work, a gift
also. Our story lights the way
by which only we together
could have come only here.

5/29/19

143

IV.

O Muse, I have not heretofore
asked for much, for it seemed
you were on my side. But now
when I am old and weary,
you bring me this travail
that I did not ask for, that might
have made me old when I was young.
I have always written beyond
my means, and I handled that
(you helping) by detours around
my ignorance. But this time
my ignorance is beating me
to the crossroads. Please help
the word I just put down
to send forth a little song
to draw out from the dictionary
another to mate with it
and produce a third. In my sore
need, I beg of your thrift, O
Muse, not a litter, but one more.

V.

Steadily and quietly the stormcloud
Moves above the hard-falling rain.

VI.

O Lord, preserve me unconsumed
by my hatred of the offices
of institutional repentance,
governmental apology,
public confession of the sins
of other people. "Flee
from the monsters of human perfection,
the whetted daggers of
the self-absolved," I counsel
myself. "Get back! Be safe
in the familiar blood-warmth
of the others who are wrong."

VII.

Things left behind should be
quiet and out of the way
and old and beautiful
as a patch of moss green
on a gray stone that the sun
touches once a day.

VIII.

And now the summer birds soon will be leaving.
And now the spiders must hurry at their weaving.

IX.

This is my method,
My more than might:
First do it wrong
Then do it right.

Thus I oppose
Myself to my wrongs,
Thus I discern
The right of my songs.

X.

"I don't know why the Lord
has been so good to me
but He shore as hell has been."

XI.

I put out seed for the birds.
At first they kept away
for fear of me. And then
the bravest came, snatched
a seed and fled, and returned
and others came. They learned
it was my peace that feast
was offered in. They came
and fed. It was the peace
of the birds I rested in.

XII.

There came a day when, still wearing
boyhood like a too-tight skin,
I was clearing a place to begin our marriage
and the long coming of age that pledged
love would require of me. And still
this river I knew from birth was passing
beside me while I worked. Resting,
watching, as the bright stream, brown
with its earthly load, flowed in the sun,
I knew in its presence all
its unending, unpausing, passing through
my people's history also passing,
my own, our own, the years to come.

XIII.

The paths went down from the road
where the fishermen walked to the river
through the horseweeds and under
the tall trees leaning over
the water, where on days away
from work and out of the sun
they thought of the baited hook,
the watched cork, and the river
that in its passing stayed.

Now they are gone, they
and the paths they made, landmarks
of a happiness that did no harm.
This place where much was given
now is pathless, given up,
the people machine-driven, burning
the world, learning nothing.

XIV.

My country, of thee I sing,
Thy history filling up
To the brim our sorrow's cup
With subtractions gathering
To a sum of screens and dope
Minus everything.

XV.

Which is the strongest part,
to be a man for women
or a woman for men? I mean
no dissolution, but love in rhyme
with the world's wholeness and healing.
Of course I know these things
as a man knows them, which
after all is half their charm.
So the heart is troubled in this age
of phantoms and screens, of falling
together, falling apart
of strangers into estrangement,
to remember there was a time
when men desired only
the incarnate women they knew
in the life of the ordinary world
where they worked in the places they lived
and ate the food they grew
from the ground that yielded also
the living water they drank.
With women they knew they entered
by familiar ways into marriage.
If they were firm enough
or fortunate enough to keep
the promise holding until death,
the forsaking of all others released
the others to be desired.
It was desire never dying
that led them through their lives,
keeping them grieved and assured
of this world's exceeding delight
that moved them by its remaining

partly beyond their reach,
partly within it. This
life, alive in the fleeting
presence of the present world,
lives yet by incarnate love.

Back when I was young
I lacked the sense and speech
to say to myself these things
that now have come in reach.

XVI.

Thy narrow gate is a wide width
thy homely creatures pass freely through,
entering this world and leaving it.
Only we unholy humans find it narrow
as we hope to slip out loaded
with rotting fruit, some we should
have eaten and given the rest away.

XVII.

The small birds come near,
nuthatch and chickadee,
almost with no fear
for I have worked quietly here,
thinking almost of peace —
this, the fifty-sixth year.

2020

I.

Here we are still on the frail
small earth wobbling in the sky,
and we are holding on
in awe and hope to the Big Brain,
our chosen almighty, while
the Six Days' Work burns
in profitable fire

until its lover's eye
looks with love upon it,
when then even the dark
begins to shine. Old
sunlight sings to the young
sun. In its lover's gaze
it becomes seen, and by his praise
begins to be as it was made.

II.

From the seed in the beginning the tree
rooted downward and rose, bringing
the dark out of the ground up
into the light. In its time it throve,
grew old, grew hollow, a living
shell holding an opening to shelter
small lives fearful of daylight
whose eyesight lights the dark.

III.

The complete breeze touches every leaf,
giving each its sound, amounting
to the one sound of many, and I am
one among the leaves, like one
among the least stars of the Milky Way,
alight, ordinary, and at home.

IV.

Old, learnéd in human failure
to love and praise enough
this present world and thus be free,
his soul, like a shirt pinned
to dry, sways in sorrow's wind.

V.

The visible bird, hidden,
fills the woods
with invisible song.

VI.

It is October, and the air cools.
The northern birds stop to feed
in our woods on their way south.
On the hillside the grass is green.
The flies that tormented the horses
have had their season and are gone.
The least asters, "farewell summer"
Art Rowanberry called them,
are whitening the fencerows, reminding me
of Art, beloved companion
of these woods and fields.
Heaven cannot be far
from here. Or maybe here
is where it is, and I have not
been there because I never
have been completely here.

VII.

A kingfisher
faster than falling
dives to the river
through the air.

In the still river
a kingfisher
rises as swiftly
out of the deep.

At the surface
the one in the air
plucks a minnow
out of the beak

of the other
in the water
and rises
alone.

VIII.

Piero

A brushstroke,
another, another,
a day and a day,
and finally Christ
stands, risen
out of his grave,
as this witness
at last has seen.

IX.

In the old days there were flocks
of chickens who lived with us
on all our farms. Back then
when Arthur Rowanberry walked

the fields in the fall of the year
and came in with his pantlegs
crusted with sticktights, he sat
on the welltop and called the hens,

the seed eaters, who came
and eagerly pecked off the sticktights.
And here we find assembled
a number of wonders to enlighten

all who hear this in years
to come: that Art knew this
was possible, that he and the hens
knew one another so well

they could so cooperate,
that this so pleased him then,
and so pleased him again
when he remembered and told us,

that it still so pleases us
when we remember. From how early
in his life did Art remember this?
Did he have it in his thoughts

.   .   .

when he endured the cutoff at Bastogne?
Oh Art, how alive you were,
who are alive forever,
when you were here with us.

X.

After his years at the work
he most wanted to do, where
he most liked to do it, with
the ones whose company he most
enjoyed, his rest came long
and deep. After love, sleep.

I.

The old project hardly had re-begun
In the season of your birth. The morning sun
Had not replaced the morning fires. The singing
Of song for song had yet to come, bringing
The couples home among the leaves. Along
The cool still-shadeless creekside lanes, among
The old year's fallen leaves, the wild woodsflowers
Had only begun to brighten the frosted hours
Of early morning. But soon the days rose
Earlier and more kind. Thus I compose
A poem to coincidence conformed.
You came. And like that year I would be warmed.

4/30/21

II.

We had the two best seats
To witness my defeats
In the battles I never won.
I forgot how they'd begun.
Seeing I had espoused
Such beauty, so aroused,
I plotted my next move,
Distractedly in love.

5/29/21

III.

It puzzled me once,
that ancient call
to ceaseless prayer.
Now I know.
Help me. Help me.
If I must stay
longer at work
give me strength.

IV.

MAURY, NELL, MAGGIE

I lived longer of course
as I was destined to do
and carried them one by one,
become at last still,
and laid them in the dark
and there left them alone
and forgot exactly where
I had placed them, for I gave
them back into the whole
world where they would always
be found, though we were lost
to one another. I knew
that I would pass near them
as I walked my rounds, and the sheep
in their rounds also would pass
near them. I planted no stone.
And they lived on in me
as I for my while in the world.
And it seems I remember the day
when at last in all the lost
places where we have waited
we wake, eternity spilling
back into time, and we rise
in our young unaching strength
that our old bodies remembered.
As if answering my call
that in time they did not hear,
they come. They lift their heads
under my hands. Speaking
all the same language now,

we forgive what we mistook.
They walk with me in the early
light across a pasture
deep in grass, where the flock
must be gathered and brought
home. "Come by!" I call
to my old companions. And so
I send them again out
into the gladness we keep
for ever in our hearts.

V.

APHRODITE (*Speyeria aphrodite*)

She disappeared among the leaves
and the shadows. I looked for her
and could not see her, though she
was nearer me than I thought.
And then she opened her wings
and the light came and met her.
She shone then with the beauty
of all things opened in welcome.

VI.

Again I have been reading
the poem "What Are Years?"
by Marianne Moore, not
to feel spoken for,
but to feel again the honor
of being so spoken to.

VII.

Coming here, he entered
his absence before he came.
He saw his country as it was,
himself not yet arrived.

He saw he had come to stay,
and he learned then to be here
by his love and work, as he
could in no other place.

Old and slow, he enters
now his absence that is
to come, the welcoming light,
the undisclosing silence.

VIII.

Propelled along the creek road
in the instrument of the fire of the end
of living things, he shuts off
the shuddering, shattering sound
that so far has shut him in
and the quiet comes down, as wide
as the sun's light and older.
Way in the distance is the call
of a single bird as yet
unanswered. He hears the whole
quiet. He hears the song.

I.

Dark and cold prevail in the wintertime.
The mind must grow old to know how nearly
complete the winter can sometimes be, how scarcely
it provides for the least birds who yet survive
the long nights and the snow and the freezing rain
to emerge again into the new dawnlight
joyous and strong. Only strength and joy
survive such nights and such days as these least
awaken to, sometimes singing their inborn songs.
The old man hears them singing, and he knows
he has outlived such joy in the flesh of his own
waking. He has known longer than the birds
the returns of the dark and the cold. He has not the birds'
sweet unknowing of the darkness made in daylight
by his own kind and their willing use of death,
the falsehood of death by which they hate this world.
But the old man knows, contrarily, that this world
was made by love. He knows it because that love
came to him one time in the person of a girl
and it abides in the girl's great-grandmotherhood.
It is with him and in him, through the dark and cold
of winter nights and human wrong, like the song
of the least birds' thanksgiving when they wake.

5/29/22

II.

By love this world was made,
by love it is known and kept,
by love we chose each other
and for ourselves this place.
The work this place has asked
we offered it in praise.

III.

Wendell Holmes Berry 1895–1944

Here is a landmark hard
to see, that in memory stands
above the horizon of this world:
the weather-stained low stone
bearing his name, the clipped
long-living grass. And here
the heart imagines him long
alone, who so gladdened in uproar
among the cronies and the women
he found in the light and air.
It was uproar, his habit, that crazed
the pride of the man who killed him.
From here then rose his silence
that enclosed us, years before
we spoke of him aloud.

IV.

Dear Ed,

In the sixty-four years we talked, how much
did we say that never would have been said
if you and I had not said it
because we were talking to each other?

Lord knows we said a plenty, some
for laughter, some for company the times
we needed each other's company, some
to tell and hear for pleasure
stories we had told and heard before, some
for the pleasure of new stories, some
in memory, where our dead friends lived.

Now half our conversation has gone
with you. The half you left is none
or less than none. I think of things
I need to ask you, or need to tell you,
and I know, and again know, and know
again, what you and I would say
now is never going to be said.

V.

At a hard task that was mine
to do but not complete
I wrought by day and in
the dark. I bore it as far
as I could go by thought
and there I made an end
of labor, and swept the room.
The light came in unblemished
by my task and then I saw
how small it was, small
in the fresh room window-lit,
smaller within the order
of the surrounding woods, the flowing
river, the greater work
coming daily to light
and also never finished.

I.

your old men shall dream dreams

I slept, and in my sleep I woke
and saw that I was coming home.
My heart rejoiced, for to come home
was ever my prayer. The way was long.
I knew at last I was returning
from my place among the dead, obeying
a voice I thought I knew. I came
to a town I seemed to recognize
by the shape of the land it stood upon.
There was a street of ugly mansions
and shops stuffed for the useless rich,
and streets of ugly factories
loud with toil of self-governed wheels
where people lived in crannies and lairs.
They were the useless poor, fugitive
and shy as mice in a barn. I heard
their small commotions, and I stopped,
troubled. But the voice said, "Come. Come on."

From there, summoned, I followed a road,
familiar in its slants and turns,
into a country I knew, my own.
But now iron and fire had passed
over it, and everything was gone:
everything above the ground,
every building, every tree,
every stone that marked our graves.
Not a flower, not a grassblade
yet lived and stained the light where once

we worked, together and apart,
in our fields, in our time. Wearing our dust,
we strove and laughed, bearing our needs
and losses, our dead living yet
among us as our stories called them
to their names. Now those fields were empty,
lifeless, the air above them void
of fragrance, flight, or song. I wept,
for I saw no sign that we who once
lived there had anywhere belonged
in that blank land. "Why," I begged
to know, "have you brought me here, where
I never willingly would have come?"

"Because," said the familiar voice,
"your life was lived and put at stake
in this world and this place as if
it and you would live forever.
Your hard virtue was desire
for everything you thought was good."

"Hold on," I said. "You call desire
a virtue, and attribute it
to me? Oh my!"

                "You're better known
maybe than you think. You served
by nature your apprenticeship
to lust, and learned enough to fear it
ever after. You learned that taking
anything you want, reduced
to your lonely wanting, brings a death
upon it, and upon yourself.

To say that you made of desire
a hard virtue is not to praise
or flatter, but merely to describe
the man you came to be. You learned,
keeping desire unspoiled by lust,
to make a sort of virtue of it,
though you remained participant in
the conflagration of the world,
the modernized original sin
that none among you has escaped
though you opposed with all your might
that sin while you committed it,
which in itself was well, there being
no escape. You argued long
enough and constantly enough
your opposition to that fire.
In that you found a kind of pleasure
which in itself was well, but not
when you enjoyed also your lust
for justice, as you hoped it was.
You tried to be a man of peace
but, as you knew, absurdly so.
At times you swallowed spite enough
to scald the guts of a peaceful man."

"I see I'm standing in the dock
and this for me is Judgment Day.
So far I find no plea to make
in my defense. Is there nothing?"

"You did not foreswear desire,
as others did, for the sake of Heaven,
or to be detached and undisturbed

by days that coming pass away,
because you liked so well to know
by desire the goods of every day."

"I thought my desire a way of love,
with love's permission to be present
with other creatures living here
in common neighborhood. I wanted
existing creatures to exist,
not to have or keep, but only
to know. So I did not desire
for the cardinal a redder red,
another or a better song.
Desiring it, I learned the world
is good, beloved of God, its maker,
breathing his breath, living his life.
Desire gives praise and thanks for life
as it is lived. It is a poise
between indifference and greed.
To live in a desirable world
without desire to live in it
condemns it by ingratitude
to its destruction and our own.
Human economy's first law
repays the world with love and thanks.
The second is to use it kindly,
in trust preserving it alive
and beautiful as it was made.
To desire the goodness of what was
as it was, I thought was life
itself, heaped up and running over.
On deathward highways that enforced
our ignorance of where we were,
I remember how I longed for home.
The happiness I knew I learned

at home. I thought it heavenly.
My gratitude for being here
gave back the joy this place gave me."

"You were the faithful husband of one
woman only in all your life,
and by your keeping faith you saw
the dwelling here you made with her
surpassing every sum and end,
in her a beauty surpassing time.
She is, you know, a giver of life.
You had from her the gift of a life
you desired and have been glad to live.
You had at last the happiness from her
of wanting only what you had.
And yet to desire everything
of this world that is beautiful
and good, though it is the world also
of death and passing time—that makes
for many partings. Desire becomes
a hard virtue when you must
relinquish everything desired.
It kept you bound in grief to all
your dead, the kin and friends by whom
you lived, your parents whose chief bequest
to you was your love for them. Think
of the dogs and horses that you loved
and have outlived and have remembered.
You may have remembered too the reasons
people famously wise advised
against desire. Yet you desired
a woman you never ceased to love,
pledged until death. And yet you saw
this world was lighted everywhere
by desirable women, given to time

like flowers in a summer field.
And you remember a woman you saw
from a passing window, a woman not young
or pretty as pretty goes, but present,
graceful, unasking, unafraid,
the only likeness of herself
only a moment seen. You loved
the small blue flowers that last a day
as if you and they would live as long
as stars. In your old age you woke
dreaming or dreamed awake the rounds
you drove your horses, beloved workmates,
mowing your grassed hillsides, each round
lifting you, the valley opening
as you mowed and rose, beautiful work,
beautiful days in memory living
once and for all their light and breath.
To rest you walked a Sabbath path
under the trees, a way never
twice the same. It disappeared
as your feet lifted, and so you walked
in the originating light,
for you also a passing thing."

"You seem to speak my mind, but with a
a warning I remember, bearing
the taint of schadenfreude, a pleasure
customarily foreseen
by those who gave the warning, who preached
the sermons answered by my boyhood
that stood in favor of the world.
'Temptations' they would have called the things
I thought so much to be desired."

. . .

"You heard, resisted, and were confused,
and yet became at last a man
of faith in the goodness and the beauty
made in the making of this world.
And now, just as the warners warned,
you have begun your journey from all
you know to all you don't. And what
are you taking with you? No pockets."

"I would take, I thought, my gratitude
for all I've loved, the presences
whose absence from this place makes it
now a Hell. Is this the final
validation of those wise heads
whose desire for nothing set them free?
But I'm not free of my desire
or of the love that I was given,
and am less free of the love I gave,
am far less free of grief for the life
and death of this once living place,
whose life I thought eternal, known
in time, and past all knowing loved.
This devastation is its end
and only worth? Can this be real?"

"Have your forgot? This is your dream,
and not the first that you have dreamed
of ruin and grief. You see this place
now as your dreams taught you to fear
it might become. While you yet lived
you saw the arrival, welcomed here
in your homeland, of ignorant money
dreaming just of itself and more
of itself. You saw waste made complete
and everlasting at the source

of your native river: mountains, forests,
the people also, overthrown
by sightless power representing
money. You saw limitless greed
crowding the world with ugliness,
armed ignorance, weapons, poisons,
bringing money to life by means
of death. And then, greatly afraid,
you felt unresting the workman's need
to make within the world's wrack
a human work that would recall
the world new made: a work of art
orderly, graceful, beautiful, good,
and true—and yet beyond the reach
of your imagination and
of any power of yours to make.
And so you desired at last to know
the world completed, not by you,
the morning of the Seventh Day."

"This world that I so loved and feared for,
in measure as I knew it, holds me
as its suckling child. And so you brought me
here, to this ruin, as punishment
perhaps because I was afraid?
To teach me now, too late, that love
so much afraid and so defiant
of a certain wisdom, was unwise?
Was wrong?"

       "This dream is only yours.
That I am in it you may thank
your hospitality. I have
been with you here in other times

when I could give you help, when you
were quiet enough, present enough,
happy enough, enough in need.
And now I am obliged to say
that you were wrong in having not
thought beyond your fear of judgment,
as if judgment only were your fate.
You did not dare believe the truth
taught by your own forgiveness, love,
and mercy for the dead, the dead
so called, who in the membership
of those you loved are living still.
And you let stand as if eternal,
ignoring all of yourself you knew,
your judgment of every one whose aims
and work and means of work opposed
the creatures and the work you loved.
You wished them in the hells they made
of places once alive, though Christ
put on their flesh the same as yours.
Because you feared it is not so,
because you feared it might be so,
you shied from knowing that above
judgment is mercy and above
mercy love. Humans have love
by being included kindly in it.
It is not theirs. So they are free
from final reckonings in which
to cage themselves. Love sets them free.

"Freely I have brought you back
to dream the ruin of all you knew
and loved: This place, your life, your dear
companions, your marriage and household

held upon the slope by work
of love. How else but by this dream
of ruin, perfect and entire,
could you have known in its full sum
your love for this place as it was
and as you hoped it might become?
Your dream of the ruin of your home land
now brings alive in you your small
share of the greater love that made
the heaven and the earth. Highest
and whole, that love is the Sabbath morning
where you at last may come to rest."

II.

I put myself in mind
of a stem of our native rye
that followed a thread of the sun
up through a pile of brush
to break out into the world
astir in full daylight
and the darkness of full night.

Acknowledgments

Author and publisher thank the editors of the following magazines for their hospitality to some of the poems that have not been previously published in a book: *Sewanee Review*, *Oxford American*, *Threepenny Review*, *Farming Magazine*, *Limberlost Review*, and *Local Culture*. And for the same hospitality, I thank my old friends Gray Zeitz and Leslie Shane of Larkspur Press.

Now I want to acknowledge some debts that are extraordinary, anything but routine.

First, my composition and editing of this book has continued my dependence of many years on the skill and patience of my beloved friend David Charlton. I know I have tried his patience with my endless changes of mind. We have spent hours on the phone paging through a manuscript to make what I call "small changes." Or I have mailed him sometimes his own copies covered with semi-legible long revisions. I have been a trial to him and he has been a lesson to me.

Next I acknowledge an unpayable debt to my friends Heather and Paul House, whose help with this book was indispensable as well as voluntary. Heather, Paul says, "spots errors at forty yards." Yes, and I suspect she can see them coming at a distance of four or five pages. Such is her vigilance that I had to develop an answering vigilance to rescue some of my pet oddities and deviations.

Index of First Lines

WENDELL BERRY, an essayist, novelist, and poet, has been honored with the T. S. Eliot Prize, the Aiken Taylor Award for Modern American Poetry, the John Hay Award of the Orion Society, and the Dayton Literary Peace Prize Richard C. Holbrooke Distinguished Achievement Award, among other distinctions. In 2010, he was awarded the National Humanities Medal by President Barack Obama, and in 2016, he received the Ivan Sandrof Life Achievement Award from the National Book Critics Circle. Berry lives with his wife, Tanya Berry, on their farm in Henry County, Kentucky.